Trust the Universe

That's where the MAGIC happens

by Vicki Williams

Copyright © 2013 Vicki Williams

First published in the USA in 2013

1st edition 25 September 2013

Revised edition 1 November 2013

2nd Edition 20 July 2020

2nd Edition Published: Red Eagle Publications

Paperback ISBN: 978-0-9876306-0-5

Hardcover ISBN: 978-0-9876306-2-9

eBook ISBN: 978-0-9876306-1-2

Cover design: PeacockDesign

Editing: Firebird Consulting Editing

Photo of Vicki: Shared Moments Photography

vickiwilliamsauthor.com.au

Dedication

This book is dedicated to the spiritual advisors I work with on a regular basis, and all those who have been instrumental in changing my life.

Preface

This book was written as part of a challenge. It happened because the Universe placed me in the right place at the right time.

This particular Monday I was full of the flu. I checked my diary to see what the rest of the week looked like and made a judgment call. I realized that, if I didn't hit this flu on the head right now, I would suffer with it for longer than I needed to.

So I took the day off work. I finished a book that had been sitting on my bedside cabinet for months. I listened to a self-guided meditation that I'd bought months before and hadn't even unwrapped the packet. I slept and then I went on Facebook where I noticed a post from Getrude Matshe, a Facebook friend from a group we are both members of. She posted a challenge for one hundred people to write a book in forty hours.

For those of you who know me, you will probably be aware that I have attempted to start writing a book many, many, many times. Usually I get the first page or chapter written and then life gets in the way. In fact, just a few months prior to this date, I had asked a friend to start a writing group with me so we could learn from each other as we write our own books, and we had had a couple of meetings. That still didn't get me writing.

So why was it that I immediately replied to Getrude, saying, and I quote: "I'm really interested, I'd love to know more about this."

Within a couple of minutes, Getrude had replied: "Can I Skype you?"

The Skype call didn't deter me in any way. In fact, it made me more determined to take the challenge. I knew this was a message from the Universe. *They* have been instrumental in creating many changes and I knew deep in my heart that *they* too wanted this book to be written. *They* had placed me in this situation today. So I committed to Getrude that I would be honored to join her challenge and, for once, I wasn't too interested in the *how*.

Acknowledgements

Special thanks to those who have provided spiritual guidance and support on my journey.

Dorothy: who gave me my very first reading in 1996. I didn't know back then that you could do readings over the phone. This was to be the first of my spiritual lessons.

Elizabeth Conway: who was the first teacher to appear when I was frustrated with my spiritual growth and hungry for spiritual guidance.

Barbara Hayward: who taught me the basics the way she was taught, and who highlighted the importance of forming a relationship with *your people* before starting to grow a spiritual foundation.

Carmel Vassallo: who taught me that meditation is the most amazing journey, where you can travel to anywhere you want, and who allowed me to constantly laugh so hard that I nearly cracked a rib.

A very special thank you to my family and friends who have believed in me and supported me in everything I do.

Your loving support is always welcomed with open arms, regardless of the distance.

My children, Daniel and Teanna: I may have been a hard-arsed mother who ruled with military precision, but when I look at you both now I am so proud of who you have become. I hope and pray that I am around long enough to share your growth through your own children.

Last, but by no means least, to Rodney, my darling husband. I bet when we met and married in 1986 you never in your wildest dreams thought our future would turn out like this. Our journey together has not been easy and I share some of our story through this book.

You have supported me through thick and thin, through projects that turned belly up, through personal and business catastrophes. You listened to me when I waffled on about spirits, guides, angels and everything else out there in the Universe as I practiced Universal principles—until you eventually believed in it yourself.

When you started believing the Universe was actually helping us, that's when the magic really started happening.

Introduction

This book takes you on a personal journey and is just one example of what is possible when you let go of fear-based practices; when you believe in yourself and trust the Universe.

The intention of the author for this book is to provide information and general guidelines of processes that worked for her.

In the event you use any of the information in this book for yourself, the author accepts no responsibility for the consequences of your actions.

Spirituality

"Recognizing and celebrating that we are all inextricably connected to each other by a power greater than all of us, and that our connection to that power and to one another is grounded in love and belonging.

Practicing spirituality brings a sense of perspective, meaning, and purpose to our lives."

Brene Brown

"Sometimes you need to distance yourself to see things clearly."

Unknown

CHAPTER ONE

Do You Hear Me?

As I sat in the darkened room, just candles flickering around me, the silence was deadly. I was on a mission, as I had been so many times before.

"Are you listening to me?" I waited. . . ."Do you hear me?" I paused, sucking in my breath, hoping, praying for an answer. "I know you're there, please help me!"

My heart was racing, I could feel it pounding harder and harder, anger was beginning to stir. That feeling I knew so well was niggling in the bottom of my gut. I listened intently for what seemed hours, but nothing, not a sound, not a murmur.

What did I expect to hear? A word, a sound, a message, what? To be honest, I didn't know. I just wanted something, something to let me know that *they* were there, that *they* had heard my plea.

I started to ask again, but stopped myself before the letters could form the words to the questions I desperately needed answered.

A message came clearly to me, one I had heard before. When you ask for help, it's like going to a restaurant and placing your order. You state what you want and let it go. You don't ask again for the same thing, you trust the chef has been given your order and that when it's cooked it will be delivered. The same goes for the Universe. You only have to ask once, and then let it go. The Universe will deliver in Divine time—if it is yours by Divine right.

I waited and waited for an answer, any answer, to the point I was bordering on losing control. I had no idea what to do; I felt lost, alone and abandoned.

"Please show me something, so that I know you are there." I waited, and strained to listen over my pounding heart. Nothing.

My doubts about my spirituality were growing stronger every day now.

Why? What had changed to make me doubt myself, doubt the Universe, doubt the messages and readings I was being given by psychics and spiritual teachers?

I got on with work, put up a mental barrier; I stopped meditating, stopped reading motivational books and stopped talking to my spiritual friends. I went into my head, and continued working all day every day. Over a few weeks I stopped smiling; I stopped laughing, I stopped being happy, and the worst thing was, *I didn't even know it*.

The clients I had booked in started to cancel. The computers would crash. I lost files, emails

Trust the Universe

bounced, and the phone stopped ringing.

One day I woke up and, for the first time ever, I didn't want to go to work; which was kind of hard as I work my business from home.

I took the day off work, put the *gone fishing* sign on the door, redirected the business phone to my mobile—and then turned my mobile off. I didn't want to be disturbed.

I went to the movies. I realized I needed to laugh again, so I immersed myself in a romantic comedy.

It was in that darkened, empty picture theatre in the middle of the day that I got the answer to the question I had asked all those weeks before.

Quite simply *they* said *Trust the Universe.*

Have you ever noticed that life's lessons are hard to accept, especially when you don't want to face the truth—ummm, so many lessons to learn!

You'd think that, at my age, I'd have learned most of my lessons in life, but alas it appears I still have plenty to learn, or maybe I'm just a slow learner.

This was my life five years ago. What happened after that day in the picture theatre started a chain of events that brings us to today; and this book will reveal how something so bad could turn out to be so beautiful.

"Every single thing that has ever happened in your life is preparing you for a moment that is yet to come."

Unknown.

CHAPTER TWO
Please Help Me

Over the next few days I felt somewhat dazed. To look at me, you would think I was in deep thought. Those who knew me sensed something was happening. It was as if they were avoiding me, not sure what to do or what to say. Truth be known, they were wondering when the bomb was going to explode, and what the fall-out would be.

I was struggling to come to terms with my thoughts and my feelings; it was as if they were travelling the same path, but in different directions. My mind was racing all over the place. I couldn't concentrate; focus was a distant word, and clarity hadn't been invented. I felt as if I was running a marathon in the wrong direction. Connections that I knew I had to make for work were passing me by, not acknowledging me, not taking me seriously. What was I doing wrong? These were warm leads; people I knew, people that wanted us to do work for them. The job was in the bag, but something was wrong. I just couldn't put my finger on it.

Picture this: it's 10:00 p.m., I'm home alone, working in my office, and the house is dead quiet —apart from the radio playing in the next room, to which I am totally oblivious.

Something happens to shift my attention from the document I was typing; what was it? I stopped typing and listened. . . . I knew something had happened. Was I still alone? Was that what alerted me? Something had caused this pattern interrupt. I strained to listen intently and heard the pitter patter of Shyla, my daughter's Burmese cat. Shyla had just woken from her after dinner nap; she roamed into the office seeking company. After jumping up onto the computer desk and doing a few laps around me seeking some affection, she eventually curled up on the chair beside me and snuggled into Misty, our Maltese.

OK, so everything is back to normal. I continued typing, but now in a less focused frame of mind. I noticed the radio was playing one of my favorite songs.

Isn't it funny that when you hear a special song that is used to promote a movie or TV program, every time you hear it, you always remember the video clip? Well, it didn't take long to realize I was humming the tune and singing along with the song.

What happened next scared the bejesus out of me. Bear in mind I was listening to the radio—not a CD, but a local radio show. I know that because, when Shyla sat on the keyboard, I shooed her off and took a moment to listen to the weather forecast for the next day.

Trust the Universe

What happened next intrigued me. The song, my favorite song played again. Weird, I thought, not sure why that had happened. I carried on typing, this time not singing along to it, but aware that it was playing.

Then it played again; this is the third time now, what the hell is going on? The fourth time it played, I started to think: this is beyond weird, this is definitely a message from above, but what were they trying to tell me? I had no idea. I hadn't had any spiritual connection for so long that I questioned what was happening. I decided to acknowledge their presence; I asked: "What was the message and who was it for?"

Then all hell broke loose. The song repeated a sentence, then repeated and repeated and repeated that sentence over and over again.

It must have been ten times. I got up, ran over to the radio and turned it off. My heart was pounding, my mind racing in every direction, asking so many questions. What did this sentence mean? I didn't understand the message. I didn't know whom it was for.

Was it the words, or some of the words? Was it the TV program that I remembered the song was written for, or was it something to do with the visuals from the promo of that TV show? I had no idea. I was left shaking all over, bewildered.

If this is how *my people* want to communicate with me I'm not sure I want to be a part of this after all. I shut the computer down and went to bed. Rodney wasn't due home from work for another hour, so I curled up with Misty in my arms, more for comfort than protection, pulled the blankets up around my neck and tried to sleep.

This was definitely a message, but what could it mean? I knew from experience the Universe can sometimes communicate in riddles and, more often than not, cryptically. Needless to say, it was a message; that gave me a tiny sliver of hope that *they* were still around guiding and protecting me.

At three that morning I awoke. I wasn't sure why, but lay in bed listening for a sign as to why I was woken. Nothing came, not a sound, not a murmur.

Am I asking the wrong questions? Maybe I am asking the wrong people. Is there a hierarchy up there? I had no idea.

I asked the Universe a different question: "I am frustrated with my spiritual journey. I am not growing in confidence. I feel stuck, and full of doubt about my physical and spiritual self. I feel nothing I am doing is working, therefore please provide me a teacher that can teach me in a way that I can understand."

"The most beautiful people we have known are those who have known defeat, known suffering, known struggle, known loss, and have found their way out of the depths.

These persons have an appreciation, sensitivity, and an understanding of life that fills them with compassion, gentleness, and a deep loving concern.

Beautiful people do not just happen."

Elisabeth Kübler-Ross

CHAPTER THREE

Is Fear Friend or Foe?

We are conditioned into fear from a very early age, and generally by our parents. Not that they are aware they do it, but whether they realize it or not, the constant barrage of their negative thoughts, barriers and actions determine the impact fear will have on our lives.

When we are children our fears are somewhat limited, but as we age and start living our lives more fully, our fears can sometimes grow to a point of overwhelm that restricts our ability to function appropriately for the situation at hand.

When I ran my life coaching practice I made a list of my client's fears, and the list read something like this:

Fear of flying
Fear of public speaking
Fear of failure
Fear of spiders/snakes or other phobias
Fear of rejection
Fear of separation

Trust the Universe

The list goes on and on. When you break it all down our fears fit into five basic categories. We aren't going into those categories in this chapter, but will focus on how these fears control us as people, and what impact that has on our life.

President Franklin Roosevelt summed it up by saying: *"The only thing we have to fear is fear itself."*

Thankfully I'm a pretty open person. I've been on an amazing journey, but it has come with a lot of life's lessons. Rodney and I married in 1986 and over the years his jobs have been made redundant a few times, and with each one of them it has meant moving.

In 1990 our son Daniel was eighteen months old and our daughter Teanna was six weeks old. We moved from Blenheim, New Zealand, to the township of Lara, Victoria, Australia, about 45 minutes south of Melbourne.

I had never been out of New Zealand before and, to be honest, I was so out of my comfort zone it wasn't funny. I am thankful that a relocation firm looked after us. They picked us up from Melbourne International Airport and drove us to our motel accommodation, and over the next month they assisted us in opening bank accounts, finding rental accommodation, and introduced us to some other Kiwis who had come over to work for the same company.

After that month we were on our own and although I was grateful for all their help and assistance, I was still panicking internally.

I didn't have any family or friends to rely on. There was no support. In those days there was only snail mail, and I would write lengthy letters home to my family describing what we experienced on a daily basis and I would wait patiently for a reply which sometimes took a couple of weeks.

I was fearful of driving. There was so much traffic compared to what I was used to and Geelong, our nearest city, was so big compared to Blenheim. I literally choked up with anticipation at the thought of driving into Melbourne. Look at it from the perspective that Melbourne held the population of New Zealand as a whole. Needless to say, during the five years we lived in Lara we only went into Melbourne CBD a couple of times.

You see, we were limited in our thoughts, size being the indicator.

It wasn't long before this new job was starting to look dodgy and our fear of losing this job became a daily talking point. The more we talked about it, the angrier we became.

Fear breeds fear—and is the breeding ground for animosity, doubt and destruction on so many levels.

At that stage, neither Rodney nor I was equipped with the knowledge we have now. We didn't see that this atmosphere was harmful not only to ourselves, but also to Daniel and Teanna, our impressionable children, who were also living in this contaminated environment. We didn't understand the extent to which we were projecting our fears onto them.

Back then, I didn't know that our thoughts create our feelings, which in turn create our reality.

I was living my life the only way I knew how,

Trust the Universe

and as openly as I could. In saying that, we did jump at the chance to move back to Christchurch, New Zealand, to once again be with family, and we lived in that cherished environment from 1995 to 2001 until we were made redundant.

I remember that day as clearly as if it was yesterday. Rodney came home from work at 6:00 a.m. pulled out a bottle of port and proceeded to drink his first glass. I took one look at what was unfolding in front of me, and asked what had happened.

Rodney looked at me with the face of a man who was coming to terms with the announcement that came out of the blue; he was motionless and drained of energy. His response was: "It's gone under, we've lost everything."

I looked at him with every ounce of courage I could muster at that moment, and said: "That's OK, which country do we move to?"

That was the attitude I needed to approach life with. I had to stand tall, to be strong, and find a solution. Rodney was too damaged to look for the positive in this situation.

I responded immediately: "Get on the phone now to everyone you know worldwide. Find out what the job prospects are and do it now before everyone else realizes there aren't enough jobs around the world for everyone affected today."

Within the week we had job offers in Tasmania, Melbourne, Sydney and Brisbane.

We didn't know which one to accept, so I rang Dorothy, a clairvoyant from whom I had received accurate readings before.

On this particular day she proceeded to tell me

Vicki Williams

"You are going back to where you have come."
"What?" I screeched, "Melbourne? No way! You never go back, you always go forward!"

She repeated Melbourne in different ways by saying things like: "You're going to the next biggest city south of Sydney and it's not Canberra," and: "You are going to work in the same building you worked in before, but it's not the same employer."

She also said another point that was very crucial to our future, although I didn't believe it at the time.

"You will work together. Rodney will invent something that will change your lives considerably."

Now, that last statement I considered to be so far left field that it was totally off the radar. I was in the medical field and Rodney was in the airline industry; there was no way we could ever work together, and why would I want to work with him anyway? What took me by surprise was that I had previously had accurate readings from Dorothy, so why now could she be so wrong?

We accepted the job with Ansett Airlines in Brisbane, mainly because it was a warmer climate, and it was closer to one of my sisters, who lived just four hours north of Brisbane.

Settling into Redcliffe, Queensland, was easy. We were now street smart, we knew what to do, and had come somewhat prepared—well, more prepared than our first move to Australia. We found accommodation and settled Daniel and Teanna into school and proceeded to get on with life.

Trust the Universe

Just three months into our life of newly acquired sun-filled days, beach walks and BBQ's our world came tumbling down around our feet.

I woke to the breaking news that Ansett had gone into liquidation and once again we were made redundant.

The news was full of it; every channel was telling the same story. Thousands of people out of work and we were just one of them. This time it wasn't so easy to find another job; the numbers of job seekers were too high. Fortunately we were open enough to look at the big picture and consider a move to another country, but even then it was limited and we didn't have the connections anymore.

The calls we did make to experts in the industry came with the stock answer "Do you really think we want you to come and work here, look at your track record. I don't want to lose my job, so no, sorry mate, but I can't help you."

The following extract is what Rodney wrote for a dear friend of ours, Helena Steel, who was a senior human resource executive for Ansett at the time of its demise. To celebrate its tenth anniversary, she wrote a book about life after Ansett. The book is titled *After Ansett - Careers of Strength and Spirit*. You can purchase this book at the website listed at the back of this book.

We were just one of many people who shared their memories of that fateful day in 2001 and what we have experienced over the following ten years.

This is Rodney's memory of the day of the collapse of Ansett in 2001, the day before his 35th birthday.

Vicki Williams

I had only been working for Ansett for 3 months after the collapse of Qantas New Zealand (formally Ansett New Zealand). I was working on the day of the collapse; we were all called into a meeting to notify us of the collapse. This was especially hard for us as we hadn't been here long enough to get any compensation and, seeing that we had lost a considerable amount of money in unpaid funds from Qantas New Zealand, neither government would help us out, so we were left to look after ourselves for quite some time.

Eventually Centrelink came to the party and provided my family a little relief. It took me nearly 9 months to get another job in an airline. In the meantime, I worked any job I could to put food on the table; as a result, my health suffered.

I blamed myself for not being able to provide for my family. I felt worthless and a failure; eventually I became depressed.

How did the change affect you?

I suppose I have become more cynical, I also believe I have become more adaptable with a willingness to try new things. I was lucky enough to get a job in the airline industry and have been promoted several times. Yes, I learned my lesson so I continued to learn and now I have two career paths that I work on a regular basis to keep up my skills.

I work both these jobs simultaneously and I also have qualifications in many different areas that I bring into both jobs.

Lessons learned and some advice for others

Having lived through the collapse of two airlines in quick succession, and moving country in an effort to find employment, what I have learned is that no job is secure and that you really need to have many streams

Trust the Universe

of income to secure your future.

Don't sit around waiting for the company to sort themselves out and don't rely on the government to assist you. Instead, jump ahead of the crowd and be prepared to move anywhere to get another position in the same industry.

Otherwise, seriously consider another career path. It is much easier to find a job while ten people from your company are looking than waiting for everyone to be looking.

Speed is of the essence, especially when large numbers of unemployed are looking and your career path is limited in this country.

Better still, be prepared and have other careers working alongside what you do now, so that in the event that you should lose your job, you will have the security of an income to fall back on.

This advice is one we have taught our children and it has served them well in carving out a more secure future.

Although we experienced painful episodes of fear-based thinking, we moved through those ten years with loads of life lessons that would ultimately shape who we were to become.

So is fear friend or foe? That's a great question, because it addresses identifying the fear and considering why it's present, what you are doing to overcome it, or staying trapped within its grasp. You do have a choice and there are plenty of programs and experts out there that can assist you in overcoming any of your fear-based practices.

It reminds me of the analogy of the rubber band; once stretched can never return to its original shape, and that is certainly true of Rodney and me.

We had been through so much in those ten years that we would never allow our future to be threatened again—or could we?

"Acknowledging the good that you already have in your life is the foundation for all abundance."

Eckhart Tolle

CHAPTER FOUR
Gratitude

Wikipedia is quoted by *officiallifebydesign.com* as stating: *Gratitude, thankfulness, gratefulness, or appreciation is a feeling, emotion or attitude in acknowledgment of a benefit that one has received or will receive. The experience of gratitude has historically been a focus of several world religions, and has been considered extensively by moral philosophers—such as Adam Smith.*

The systematic study of gratitude within psychology only began around the year 2000, possibly because psychology has traditionally been focused more on understanding distress rather than understanding positive emotions. However, with the advent of the positive psychology movement, gratitude has become a mainstream focus of psychological research. The study of gratitude within psychology has focused on the understanding of the short-term experience of the emotion of gratitude (state gratitude), individual differences in how frequently people feel gratitude (trait gratitude), and the relationship between these

Trust the Universe

two aspects.

I wonder if you realize just how powerful gratitude is? I am familiar with quite a few people that practice gratitude as part of their business. Some have written books on the subject, others use this tool to coach their clients into a much more abundant lifestyle.

Although my spiritual journey is still on the ground floor, so to speak, every day I learn the secrets of how all the principles work together.

Gratitude is by far one of the first lessons and once you master it and use its power to the best of your ability, you will notice a massive difference in yourself and the environment you live and work in.

It becomes one of those tools that have a flow on effect, the synergy of like attracting like. So it stands to reason the more grateful you are for what you have, then the more the Universe will give you to be grateful for.

As for myself, I had been told many, many times: *When you go to bed at night, write down a list of things you are grateful for.* That's all you have to do, nothing more.

If you want to see improvements in your life then do this exercise. Every night write down a list of things you are grateful for. Below are some examples.

I am grateful for the sun that warms my body

I am grateful for the rain that waters my garden and vegetables

I am thankful that I have an abundance of clean water to drink

I am grateful two new clients chose to work with us

Vicki Williams

this week

I give thanks to the person who drove out of the perfect parking space today

I am thankful my daughter is cooking tea for me tonight

I am grateful Rodney was not seriously hurt when he fell off his pushbike

I am grateful for the unconditional love of my pets

I appreciate the kisses and cuddles from my grandson

I give thanks for the abundance of fresh food

I remember the many times I have started this exercise. I would grab a notebook and put it beside my bed and each night I would write five things I was grateful for that day. To be honest, I'd do that for a couple of weeks and then life would get in the way. I'd use the notebook for something else, or someone would use the notebook and not put it back beside the bed. Ultimately, over time, I would forget to continue.

My very dear friend Derek Barker who wrote the book: *A Gift of Gratitude* also produced CD's on gratitude. What I am truly grateful for is that Derek has for sale on his website a gratitude journal. This gratitude journal has blank pages where you can write what you are grateful for and I continue to record my list every night. I put it down to the fact that this is a designated journal and I don't use it for anything else. It has its purpose and I can see it or find it at a glance. Problem solved, for me, anyway. It may just answer your prayers as well. Certainly worth a try if it keeps you in a grateful state.

Gratitude is just one of the tools and strategies

Trust the Universe

that I use to bring more abundance into my life. I do practice gratitude on a daily basis, and for those of you who know me you will be familiar with a set of words I use abundantly. They are: *thank you, thank you, thank you*. I say it in three's because I was taught it has more power than just saying it the once.

You may like to start with just this one tool. For everything that happens, as soon as you receive it, say: *thank you, thank you, thank you* out loud, and feel the gratitude.

In no time at all it will become a habit that will invoke more things to be grateful for.

Another tool that I use is benevolent outcomes. I learned all about them from Tom T Moore, author of *The Gentle Way*. This book is for people of all faiths and beliefs—the only requirement is a basic belief in angels. Tom's easy to read and easy to digest practical tools within this book have given me great insight into what is possible when you ask.

I use benevolent outcomes most days. The great thing about them is you only have to ask once, and let it go—the Universe will do the rest.

The following benevolent outcomes are adaptations of ones quoted in Tom's book.

When I hear that someone is applying for a job I always ask them to say this as they hit the send button or drop their application into the post box:

"I request a most benevolent outcome that this application reaches the person who is open-hearted and can see that I am the perfect person for this position and that the outcome be even more beneficial than I had hoped for. Thank you, thank you, thank you."

If they get an interview I ask them to say:

"I request a most benevolent outcome for being hired with this employer for the perfect position for my growth and expertise, and that I stay employed here as long as I want. Thank you, thank you, thank you."

How about a benevolent outcome for those times when you know you are going to be late for an appointment?

"I request a compression in time until I reach my destination and a most benevolent outcome to find a perfect parking space as I arrive safely. Thank you, thank you, thank you."

I don't ask the Universe *how* or *when* they should arrive, as the Universe will deliver when I am ready, if it is my Divine destiny. I appreciate and respect that this is how it happens.

The Universe calls the shots. If you don't know about Divine Time you soon will, as I refer to it often as part of one of life's lessons I needed to experience in this lifetime.

I trust that these tools can be of benefit to you and that you use either or both of them to increase your abundance.

"It's not about how to achieve your dreams.
It's about how to lead your life.

If you lead your life the right way, the karma
will take care of itself.

The dreams will come to you."

Randy Pausch

CHAPTER FIVE
Choices

I started my personal development journey in 2006. I was not happy in my personal life, communication with Rodney was almost non-existent and Daniel and Teanna were teenagers bordering on young adults. Oh, to experience the joys of raising teenagers! Many emotions, fears and frustrations come flooding back as I think about it. Thankfully those days are a distant memory and I am lucky enough to say we survived with not much to worry about. Of course, at the time it was an entirely different ball game.

Coming from a fairly naïve background, non-existent where drugs were concerned, I had no idea what to expect, what signs to look out for, or what to do even if I noticed any unusual habits forming in the kids.

Rodney and I were faced with a choice; did we want to continue to parent in a way that was giving neither of us any satisfaction or look for another way, an alternative. It was the lesser of two evils. Did we want to parent the easy way or the hard way? Did we want to bury our heads in the sand and pretend that life was a bed of roses or could we find other ways of dealing with the situations we were facing with our teenage children?

Rodney and I attended a course the high school ran on how to communicate with young adults and, in all honesty, we did learn a few things. In a way it was good that we did the course with other parents, because it uncovered two things. It made us realize we were not going through this stage of parenting alone and we soon realized that our kids were not as bad as we had first thought.

I remember Rodney saying to the teacher at the completion of the course: "Thanks for the opportunity to learn more about our children and what they are facing in today's society. Could you please tell me when you are running the course for the kids to learn about what we parents are facing in today's society?"

Funny how the school had never even contemplated running a course to signify how hard it was for us to parent teenagers.

It was at this time that I was really frustrated with being a parent, mother and wife. I knew something had to change, but I didn't know what.

Work was OK. I loved my job and was really good at it, but I also knew it was a dead-end job with no prospects.

I wasn't being heard at work and, because I was so efficient at what I did, I was continually being taken advantage of, being given more and more work that others doing the same job as me didn't get done. This angered me, as I saw it as a punishment.

Why should I have to do their work because they were incompetent, didn't have time management skills and basically were useless at their job? Why did I have to do it for them?

This really bugged me and when the employer offered us some additional training I jumped at the chance to learn something new. The course was self-paced and could take a year to complete, but I had it finished within five months.

This had started a hunger in me for more knowledge; more skills and, for once, I saw that maybe there was a future. Not sure what, but I was now open to taking risks.

Over lunch in the cafeteria the conversation was around our future and where we saw ourselves at retirement. I was only 45, so didn't see it as too much to worry about at that stage.

The question that was posed to the group was: "What would you like to do when you retire, do you want to work or rest?"

Gosh. What did I want to do when I retired? I had no idea.

Ultimately, I would like to rest, sit back and enjoy myself, but reality had a different message.

We had been hit pretty badly with being made redundant so many times and, although we were on our way up in terms of financial security, it would still take a hell of a lot to be financially secure enough to rest during retirement.

The hard fact was that, right then at that moment, I would have to work during retirement;

Trust the Universe

so, seriously, what would I like my job to be?

Would I still be in this same job, only more frustrated than I am now? Would I be working for someone else? What if I was unable to work due to accident or sickness, what then?

I meekly replied: "I have no idea what I want to do. I'm not sure I have the skills to keep me employed during retirement."

A very dear friend said: "Jump on the internet and start looking, the perfect job will find you."

I went home that night and did just that. I jumped on the Internet to search for possibilities.

What could I do with the skills that I already possessed? I searched and searched, not finding anything that tempted me, until eventually I stopped focusing with tunnel vision and took a wider look at what was in front of me. It was then that I saw those ads on the right hand side. Normally I am not drawn to them; normally I don't even glance at them, but today they were calling me. Today I noticed for the first time the power of advertising.

What was flashing like a beacon on that left hand side was an advert to be a Life Coach. Interestingly enough Rodney and I had won a free life coaching session some years earlier and although I was familiar with the concept, I just didn't know exactly what being a life coach entailed.

The search for me was becoming more targeted. I wanted to know more about what a life coach did, what qualifications did they need, were there training programs, what did it cost and more importantly, was this something that I could do?

Vicki Williams

I sent off emails to the training establishments I could find in Melbourne and within a few hours had an invitation to attend an information session at The Coaching Institute from none other than Sharon Pearson, the founder. Back then, Sharon was still working in the business, growing it, building the foundation for the empire it is today.

Rodney accompanied me to this session. We pulled up outside her Port Melbourne terrace home. Sharon had just bought the terrace next door and was in the process of converting it to office space from which to run the business.

A funny thing happened to me as I opened the front door—I experienced an overwhelming feeling of déjà vu.

I had been here before and that certainly became evident when Sharon yelled out from the front offices: "I'm just photocopying some paperwork, so please make yourself a coffee and I'll be with you in a minute."

I walked straight into the kitchen; I knew exactly where the cups, tea and coffee were and proceeded to make a cup for everyone patiently seated waiting for the session to begin.

That night in July 2006 I knew my life was about to change, but I didn't know to what extent. This was something I could do; life coaching was something I could take into retirement; life coaching was something I could do anywhere in the world. I suddenly realized that I didn't have to be stuck in an office working for someone anymore. I could work for myself. I could choose my clients, I could choose the hours I worked and I could choose where I wanted to work. For the

Trust the Universe

first time in my life I could make choices for me. I didn't have to think about the wellbeing of everyone else.

The Universe had started the ball rolling, and roll it was going to do.

As we drove home that night, I was over the moon with excitement; my mind was in overload taking in all the information that Sharon had delivered.

Eventually I noticed an eerie silence from Rodney and wondered what was causing it.

My immediate thought was, I have found something I really want to do and yes it costs a lot of money.

I knew Rodney well enough to know that he was probably adding up all the costs and deciding we couldn't afford it. He just didn't know how to tell me.

"OK, so what's the problem?" I asked.

After a moment or two he sheepishly responded: "I know you want to do this, well—I err—I—phew . . . I want to do it as well."

I looked at him, dumbfounded; where the hell had that come from I wondered.

Although he was driving, I sensed he was struggling to stay focused on the road. "You want to be a life coach? What are you going to do, give up work?" This sounded like madness. Didn't he realize for once in my life this was about me? This was my future, my way out of the dead-end job that frustrated the living shit out of me. This was my choice; all I wanted of him was to stand by me, to support me like I had supported him all our married life, and especially through the redundancies over all those years.

Then it hit me. He had suddenly realized I was about to embark on a journey. We had no idea what the future would hold and, if he didn't join me, he would be left behind. What was possible or what could happen scared him more than coming out of his comfort zone and learning to communicate not only with me, but with other people as well.

I reminded him that life coaching was about working on yourself, improving yourself, getting rid of fears and phobias, then using those skills to help your clients.

He said: "Yes, I know, I was there with you, remember. I heard what Sharon had to say."

I waited a moment before I stated the obvious, well the obvious for me.

I wanted Rodney to know the full implications of what he was getting into. "You realize that you will have to get rid of your shit! You realize you will have to talk to people you don't know! You realize you will have to listen to people's problems! You realize you will have to help people! You realize that to do all that you will have to communicate!"

"Yes, I know that!" he snapped back.

I responded: "Well, how the hell are you going to do that when you can't even talk to me?"

"I'll just have to learn then, won't I?" he replied, spitting the words out with a vengeance.

I knew I had pushed the boundary too far; best to shut up and let him ponder this in his own way.

We both became life coaches and, to be perfectly honest, it saved our marriage. Thanks to The

Trust the Universe

Coaching Institute and to Sharon and her amazing coaches who trained us over the next few years.

Rodney did learn to communicate and now he's nothing like he was. He has a newfound confidence about himself, he speaks up for those being taken advantage of, or who haven't the confidence to speak for themselves. He stands tall in his own power and he cares about people now.

I have to say I am really pleased he realized that night in July that a change was coming, and I am thrilled he wanted to be a part of it.

Was life coaching easy? Hell no! There were SO many choices to make. Was I going to freely get rid of all the crap I was carrying around with me? I had loads of fears that were ingrained so deep I wondered how I'd ever get rid of them.

Was I good enough to be a life coach?
What do I know anyway?
Would the client listen to me?
Would I even get a client?
Would I be able to help them?
How much do I charge them?
Where do I go to find clients?
What if I was a failure?
How do I run a business?

I analyzed the situation so much I went into overwhelm and then went about finding proof that all those concerns were in fact the truth. Fear was keeping me small; fear was keeping me a prisoner within.

Like most things you do in life, you don't know what you don't know until someone tells you. This is most definitely the case with life coaching.

Like an onion, the more we peeled away the

layers of who we were, the more we realized we needed fixing. Don't get me wrong, this is a good thing. This journey into oneself is what makes a more in-tune person and life coach. Well, that's my opinion.

I made personal choices during those early life-coaching years that I stand by today; not that everyone else sees these changes the same way I do. They were important to me then, and they still are today.

Over time, I noticed a difference. Rodney was less stressed and for the first time in our married life we talked and talked. We shared a common interest other than the children.

It was my perception that Daniel and Teanna appeared to be different, happier and more content. There was harmony in the home and I was beginning to feel I was where I needed to be, and I was happy about that.

Our life coaching business didn't last long; it took three years until we realized the money was in business coaching. The only problem with that was neither Rodney nor I had a business background and struggled to implement a business strategy.

The Universe came to the rescue, and placed Rodney in the *right-place-at-the-right-time* to meet a person who was to become a mentor that would see what we couldn't see about ourselves.

Over time, this mentor, sensing we were pure of heart, connected us to other business owners who opened doors for us.

It was through this mentor that our coaching business morphed into something completely

Trust the Universe

different.

He was quick to work with our anything-is-possible, can do attitude and with baby steps he built up skills we didn't even know we had. This in turn enabled us to create our own video production company.

Remember back at the start of this book I mentioned Dorothy, a clairvoyant that I had called when Rodney was made redundant in New Zealand on 21 April 2001.

On that particular day she proceeded to tell me: "You are going back to where you have come, back to Melbourne."

Twelve years later and I am now starting to piece it all together. She was right, after all those years of disbelieving her! We did eventually end up back in Melbourne; even though we took the job in Brisbane with Ansett, only to lose it three months later, and then went to a job in Adelaide, and eventually back to Melbourne to work in the same building Rodney had worked in years before, but this time with a different employer, just exactly as Dorothy had predicted.

We started working together as life coaches and then together in our video production company.

The Universe had given us a choice and we had chosen it our way. Ironically, the end result was the same, only our way took us on more of a detour. How were we to know that the Universe would bring us back on track when we both needed it?

How wrong was I to have doubted Dorothy?

When Rodney and I first opened our coaching business, we asked ourselves: "Why—why take the risk?"

We put together a list of the reasons why we wanted to run our own business.

On the whiteboard beside where I write this book in big bold letters is our list.

Lifestyle – the ability to choose our destiny.

Work hours to suit – the ability to choose the hours we want to work.

Work together – the freedom to choose whom we want to work with, clients, contractors and crew.

Make money – the ability to earn an income that sustains our lifestyle and the freedom to choose the projects we work for charity.

Travel – the ability to choose where and what projects we want to do. This has seen us travel and work in Thailand, L.A, Hong Kong, Brisbane, Canberra, Perth and most of Victoria.

Fun – we have worked on some amazing projects. Each day is a different day in our line of work.

Variety – one day we could be filming a web video, a short film, or editing.

Choose our destination – the choice to plan and be in control of our future, our way.

I am pleased to say that this list only needs a little more work to be 100% congruent as our business model.

Fun—we could put more fun into each day. We do tend to get bogged down some days.

"Meditation is all about the pursuit of nothingness. It's like the ultimate rest.

It's better than the best sleep you've ever had. It's a quieting of the mind.

It sharpens everything, especially your appreciation of your surroundings.

It keeps life fresh."

Hugh Jackman

CHAPTER SIX
Meditation

Meditation means many things to many people; it is bigger than just you and me. Globally, different faiths meditate for different reasons and the meditation described in this book is my own personal experience of meditation and relates to where I am in my spiritual development.

Way back in 2004 I worked with a wonderful woman, Terri, with whom I connected on a spiritual level. She was further along her spiritual journey and, like a sponge, I would listen intently to her stories about spirits wanting to speak through her, and how scared she was of allowing them to. The battles she was facing within herself at that time put a whole new meaning around the word *choice*. She knew eventually she would become a channel, but she wasn't ready and, judging by the way she was feeling, I doubted it was ever going to happen.

She asked if I wanted to attend a meditation class at a spiritualist church that she attended. It

Trust the Universe

was a no brainer. Hell yes, of course I did, but I wanted support, so I took Rodney with me.

My very first experience with spirituality was just after my father died in 1975. My mother, older sister and I were drawn to a spiritual gathering being held at a community hall. From memory, I had read about it in the local newspaper and together we bravely attended. Having absolutely no idea what was happening, we didn't speak to anyone and I am not sure anyone spoke to us. We were just three in a room full of people, all wanting desperately to get a message from our loved ones that had passed over.

In 2006, thanks to my connection with Terri, I found myself standing outside a spiritualist church with its quaint little picket fence, wondering what was going to become of me once I entered. Anticipation and fear make a strange combination, but that night I couldn't determine which emotion was going to take first place.

As we entered, I noticed the chairs were placed in an oval shape around the room. Terri was there, and she introduced us to the people present. Thankfully, it was only a small gathering. Dorothy, who ran the meditation, spent a few minutes with Rodney and me, explaining what would happen from start to finish, reassuring us we were in a safe, controlled environment. She grabbed us a glass of water each and invited us to sit down. She placed us beside some of the more advanced participants for added support. The lights were dimmed and the meditation began.

The beautiful soothing music slowly comforted my stressed body, and the delicious smell of incense filled my nostrils and calmed me as Dorothy spoke in a beautiful, hushed tone that relaxed every part of my body.

As I drifted off with the music, I struggled to follow the journey Dorothy was taking us on. I felt so relaxed and at peace and it took me completely by surprise as I felt this drawing sensation that I can only describe as being sucked into a vacuum. It wasn't an uneasy, unpleasant experience, but instead peaceful and, without opening my eyes, I realized I was looking down on the people in the room. I must say it was both weird and not, at the same time. I had no idea how I got there, how long I had been there or what I was there for.

All I remember was Dorothy shaking me awake, repeating my name again and again. "Vicki, come back, Vicki, wake up, Vicki it's safe to come back, come back now."

When I came to I wondered what had happened and why everyone was looking at me. I could sense a general concern for me, but wasn't sure why. Dorothy explained that I had been astral travelling. Of course, I had heard of it, but had no idea what it was or why I had done it. I couldn't remember going anywhere and I began wondering if I had done this before.

I asked Dorothy if it was possible I would astral travel if I meditated at home. Dorothy explained how to surround myself in blue light and ask Archangel Michael for protection.

I left meditation that night with a longing to know more. Who was Archangel Michael? What did he do and how was he going to protect me?

Trust the Universe

The fear of not knowing what I would find if I travelled without protection or if I forgot to surround myself with blue light before I went to bed at night was weighing me down. The uncertainty of the danger I could expose myself to was too great to face and so I did what I knew oh so well. I put up a barrier and blocked spirituality from my mind. I didn't want to go there, it was just too scary.

Meditation raised its ugly head again when I started coaching. I was studying so hard, working full time and creating the coaching practice in my spare time. I started to coach my clients on work/life balance—only to realize I wasn't practicing it myself; in fact, from where I was sitting, the word *balance* hadn't been invented.

I was attending training sessions nearly every weekend and completing homework all night every night.

It was bedlam. I was tired, stressed and it wasn't long before overwhelm was my constant companion.

While studying the Wheel of Life I realized that, to teach this strategy to my clients, I needed to be experiencing it firsthand. It was evident that I needed to find balance in my life, so I reworked my diary and allowed time for me. I found myself a wonderful remedial masseuse who pounded away my tension and when I scheduled my hair appointments, I would book it for mid-afternoon and take the rest of the day and night off.

Rodney and I used to enjoy our date nights or weekends away, but with us being so busy working and growing the coaching practice these treats had slipped away, so I made sure I programmed them into the diary. Three times a year we would go away for a long weekend and once a month we would go out for dinner and catch a movie or something else where we could just veg out.

The training sessions—for coaching, NLP and speaking from stage that Rodney and I attended with The Coaching Institute and then with Chris Howard—gave us the ability to bounce ideas off other coaches that we knew. It was at one of these sessions that I mentioned my stress levels and lack of balance, to which I was told I needed to meditate.

I admitted I was too scared to meditate and they recommended I go online and buy one of Louise Hay's meditations. This was the first I'd heard about Louise Hay, so I jumped online and was gob-smacked by the variety of products she had available. Like a pig in heat I bought nearly everything I thought would help me. Anything that sounded like it would give me some clarity on how to meditate.

Not satisfied with just Louise Hay, I wanted more. I found Doreen Virtue and Diana Cooper and became introduced to the Archangels through their meditations. Then I found The Secret, and the Law of Attraction opened up another series of learnings for me.

It suddenly hit me that I had control of my destiny; my life could be whatever I chose it to be.

The coaching trainings took on a whole new meaning for me now. I was focused on my future, or what I thought I wanted my future to be.

Trust the Universe

I started listening to guided meditations every night before I went to sleep and also during the day if I felt I was getting too stressed. These meditations allowed me to unwind and focus on me; they were a great source of relaxation. I felt safe and in control as I listened to different masters.

I was back in control again and everything was in order. I felt a million dollars, and business was booming. My clients were growing in number and they were making great progress with redeveloping and reshaping their lives.

Rodney was doing an exceptional job with his clients and he was enjoying getting out and networking. Overall, life was pretty damn good.

A client of mine at the time had suggested that I start self-meditating and told me that she had learned by staring into the flicker of a candle; you clear your mind until you think about nothing but the candle flame.

I was eager to get this down pat. The need for me to meditate by myself and not through a guided meditation meant so much to me. I was so grateful that someone had given me an insight into how to transition from one to the other that, as soon as she had left the office, I turned off the phone and lit the first candle I could find.

I made myself as comfortable as possible and stared into the flame. Thoughts took over; my mind was like Grand Central Station. I suddenly thought of all the things I needed to get done. "Focus, Vicki, focus."

I stared into that candle deeper and deeper. I squinted my eyes in an effort to see more clearly.

Vicki Williams

After what seemed like forever I decided that was a waste of time, or maybe I was doing it wrong. But then, what was I expecting to happen?

I left it a few days and tried again, this time allowing myself longer to clear my mind, but the same thing happened. As soon as I slowed down my breath I would be flooded with thoughts of things I had to do.

The shrill of the phone broke my focus and I admitted defeat once again.

Determined to crack this baby, I waited until I was home alone and turned the phone off. This time I was going to make it happen. To set the mood I listened to a guided meditation first to totally relax, and then I grabbed as many candles as I could find and placed them around me.

I took slow deep breaths, and focused in on the flame of the candle, and each time my mind wanted to fill with thoughts I tried my damn hardest to let them go. I was going to win if it was the last thing I did, and just to make sure I set the timer for five minutes.

I sat there intently looking into the flame and waited for something to happen, anything. Not knowing what I was waiting for, I soon became bored and, without realizing, I allowed my mind to run wild. Within a few minutes I was more intent on relaxing in the peaceful ambience of the room than staring into that damn candle flame.

What pissed me off even more was the realization that I couldn't do it, it wasn't working and I didn't know what else to do.

I doubted that I had any spiritual gifts within me at all. I couldn't even meditate by myself!

Trust the Universe

What kind of a loser was I?

So I stopped trying to do it by myself and over time I even stopped listening to self-guided meditations as well; after all, what was the point?

My spiritual journey went on holiday and I went back to work.

You probably guessed it didn't take long before I was back to the grindstone and work was once more a chore.

Whether it was a blessing or not, the GFC hit and all but one of my coaching clients decided their money was too precious to spend on their personal development. They needed that money to pay the bills and almost within a month I was struggling to make ends meet.

"We learn something from everyone who passes through our lives.

Some lessons are painful, some are painless but all are priceless."

Unknown

CHAPTER SEVEN

The Beauty Within

We knew the big money was in business coaching. The trouble was neither of us came from a business background and we didn't know where to start. We didn't know how to talk to corporate people; they spoke a whole different language.

Things looked pretty grim for our coaching practice and we had no idea what we were going to do.

Rodney came racing home from a networking event on a real high. He'd met some amazing people and one person in particular, Gary Schuller, really connected with him.

Rodney could tell me that Gary introduced him to some members of the network that he felt could be of benefit to us.

What took us completely by surprise was that Gary phoned us later that day to see what Rodney had thought of the networking event and also to find out more about our business and how he could help us. He said he was pretty well connected and could introduce us to people where our services could be of benefit to them.

After speaking to Gary we both looked at each other and agreed that this felt like the right place to be.

We believed the Universe had placed us at this point for a reason.

We assumed it was for the business coaching connections.

Isn't it funny how you think your life is going in one direction, but the Universe has a totally different plan! The only problem is that when you get close to figuring out what the Universe has in store for you it is so far left field that you question it.

We joined Gary's networking event because it felt right and we didn't really know what else to do.

We became very close personally and Gary got to know us really well.

The great thing about Gary was he could see in us what we couldn't see in ourselves. He saw skills and attributes that we didn't even know we had. He believed in us when we didn't. He backed us and was prepared to give us a go when others wouldn't and he respected our core values.

Gary ran a monthly networking event in Melbourne, and—as the Universe places us in Divine time—we just happened to be at Gary's office the morning he got a call from his audio visual company saying they couldn't do the AV for his event that was due to happen in two days.

Gary got off the phone really pissed, as you can imagine. "Where am I supposed to find another

Trust the Universe

audio visual company to put on my event at such short notice?" He had a look of disappointment and defeat. "What am I supposed to do now?"

"I'm sure I can do it for you," said Rodney. "Our son is a disk jockey in his spare time so I am sure he has everything we need to put this gig on for you."

"Are you sure? I'd be really grateful if you could," Gary asked cautiously.

"I'll call you tonight and let you know one way or the other," replied Rodney.

We did the audiovisuals for that event. The conversation that followed that day was sort of like this: "Why am I paying an AV company $1,500 for a few hours work when we could do it ourselves, that is if you guys want to continue to be my AV crew?"

Over the next year Rodney and I helped him open twenty networking events around Australia. This didn't come easy to us, but we made a commitment to Gary and ourselves and we did everything in our power to make it happen.

We had no idea who would be the territory leader at these new networks and as we physically made the lighting stands to light the stage and banners, we devised a way to make the lighting stands light enough for a smallish woman to erect by herself. We would supply each new territory with everything to conduct their event from an audiovisual perspective, so that they didn't need to use any of the venue's equipment. Because this was provided in a rather large metal box it made flying rather awkward. This meant we drove to all the destinations, which was OK, but took a lot more planning.

I remember when we were opening an event in Canberra. Rodney was still working full time for Qantas and building up his coaching clients in his spare time.

This particular day he was working day shift and finished at 3:00 p.m. He came home, we loaded the car and drove to Canberra, some 650km, taking about eight hours.

We arrived in Canberra just after midnight and, thankfully, they allowed us into the room to set up for the event starting at 7:00 a.m. We finished setting up the room about 2:00 a.m. and grabbed 40 winks. We greeted everyone as they arrived for the networking event and enjoyed a wonderful morning. We were packed up and ready to leave by 11:00 a.m. and hit the road back to Melbourne arriving in time for Rodney to go back to work for his normal ten hour shift.

Some people would see that as being dedicated, some would view it as crazy, stupid; either way they are probably right. We did what had to be done in the only way we knew how.

That year taught us lots of life's lessons. We learned so much about ourselves individually and as a couple. I remember Rodney saying as we were driving to one of these networking events: "This is the most rewarding part of the job, because we get to spend all these hours together, just you and me. We are stuck here in the car and it's about the only time now when we can get to talk, discuss and plan our future."

When we travelled to these networking events we would have our business meetings, work out our strategy forward, make plans about the future, design and develop what we were going to do next and how we would make it happen.

They were certainly very special times. Was it easy? Hell no! Would I change any of it? Probably not.

My highlight would be the people that we met over that time. Most of those people came to us with the same open heart that we operate from.

This is where we learned about filming. Gary implemented a membership package and offered a three minute video clip of their business to put on their website. Another member used to film these, but got so busy with his own business that he told Gary he was no longer available. So Gary asked us if we could film them while we were at the event, you know—kill two birds with one stone, so to speak.

We are very much go-getters: *say yes and figure out how later* kind of people. So, of course, we said: "Yeah, why not." We turned up to the first thing we filmed with our little handycam and soon realized this was just not going to do. So we researched video cameras and tried to work out all the other things we'd need to make this a more professional job.

It was about this time that I was introduced to an amazing woman, Jacqueline Bignell, who'd received a message from the Universe—*her people*—that she was going to make a movie. Her vision is to collect six thousand people globally to co-create the movie *The Difference: opening humanities heart*. When I heard this, it was a no brainer that I had to be a part of it.

Vicki Williams

Jacqueline was in the same predicament. To film this project she would need cameras and to learn how to use them. So as collaborators we learned together about the technology side of film and video.

We learned from each other and I am proud to say that on a very auspicious day in Melbourne that we filmed the first of the Melbourne Difference Collaborators interviews. It was a stinking hot 43-degree day and we filmed in an average sized motel room. The room was filled with a host and two or three guests, three cameras, lights, and about four other crewmembers. We were jammed in like sardines and from memory I think we filmed about forty interviews that day.

Thankfully, it didn't take long for us all to be working together like a well-oiled machine. Surprisingly, at the end of the day some of the collaborator's had hung around to give us all shoulder and foot massages, which were so gratefully accepted. During the day not one of us complained about the heat, the cramped conditions, nothing. We were there because of our love and support for Jacqueline.

A couple of months later, at a meeting with some of The Difference collaborators, I met Debra Wylde, she was down from Sydney and meeting her was my first introduction to working with vibrational energy I'd never heard of such a thing.

Being in a room with such openhearted people and such energy was exactly the right place for me. This is where I wanted to spend my days; these were the people I wanted to work with, it

Trust the Universe

just felt right.

It was at this time Rodney and I made a decision to branch out on our own and Rovick Productions was born.

"Begin today.

Declare out loud to the universe that you are willing to let go of struggle and eager to learn through joy."

Sarah Ban Breathnach

CHAPTER EIGHT

New Beginnings

Because of our filming of The Difference interviews that stinking hot day in Melbourne, we got to know one of the collaborators, Heather Yelland, a whole lot better.

We were honored when she asked us to film her personal development retreat in Thailand; it was a ten-day trip to film a five-day workshop.

Just before we were about to leave to go to Thailand, I received an email out of the blue about a directors training course—for some reason I was drawn to this. It ran out of Melbourne the week we were going to holiday in Thailand, immediately after filming Heather's retreat.

Until now, Rodney and I were doing every part of film and video ourselves; when we looked at the list of crew in the course notes, we were somewhat curious about what they did. We were even unsure about some of the equipment they talked about. So curiosity won and we enrolled into the course, mainly to quench our own curiosity more than anything else.

We loved the weeklong directors' course; it covered every aspect of making a short film, from writing the script to editing the end footage.

We called our directors course short film *Kleptomania*. It's a story about a jewel thief that I helped co-write.

The next major project came from Debra whom I had met that day at The Difference meeting. We were at Port Douglas, Queensland, for our daughter Teanna's wedding. Debra rang and asked if we would consider being her film crew for an online TV reality show she was putting together.

An online TV reality show! Us to be her film crew? Hell yeah! Like I had to even consider it.

The details were foggy as it was still conceptual.

The bottom line was she wanted to take twenty businesses from where they were right at that moment to a one million dollar business in a year by using vibrational energy and universal principles; the concept of bringing spirituality into business.

With Debra living in Sydney and us in Melbourne, I asked where this was all being filmed; after all, I still had a business to run. Sure we could go to Sydney once a month to film it, no problems.

Debra said she was heading off to Turkey for a few weeks and we'd talk when she got back, which was fine because, after all, I was at my daughter's wedding. What she did ask was if I could think of any people in business that would like to take on this challenge.

Trust the Universe

I was ecstatic and fearful at the same time. Wow, what an honor, what a gift. Filming a TV reality series was something that just didn't happen to most people, so I was quick to relay this message to Rodney and my family who were over from New Zealand for the wedding.

I couldn't wait for Debra to come back and talk more about this show. I had mentioned it to a few of my close friends and they were really interested.

When I next spoke to Debra I asked my long list of questions and mentioned that quite a few of my business friends were interested. I passed their details to Debra who went about interviewing them for the show.

The more I talked to Debra about the show, the more I wanted to be a participant. Of course, we would still film it, but I wanted the opportunity to be one of the businesses to go from where we were right then to a million dollar business in a year. Let's be honest, who wouldn't?

She allowed us to be one of the businesses as well as the film crew. Thankfully, we had been training up our son, Daniel, behind the camera and so Rodney and Daniel were the crew for the online TV reality show The OMM Project.

Because all the participants ended up coming from Melbourne it was obviously easier for Debra to come to Melbourne once a month to film than us all going to her in Sydney.

We called a meeting with all interested participants; there were eight of us at that first meeting, most of whom had been a connection from me. That meeting was held in our front lounge, which was to become the film studio.

On that first day we all went before the camera to introduce ourselves and talk about our thoughts on turning over a million in a year. What did that look like to us and what would we have to overcome to get there? What product or service could we introduce to make that kind of money?

When the question was asked: "Vicki, how could Rovick Productions make a million dollars?" I remember Debra looking at me and saying; "Why don't you just make a movie?"

I shrugged my shoulders. My response at the time was: "Not that I have ever done it, but to make a movie takes money, not make money, unless of course you are a really skilled big-named director or producer."

"Yes,—but what's stopping you?" Debra asked.

To be honest, I had never considered making a movie. We were still, in my opinion, learning skills and knowledge. Even after doing the directors course, we hadn't contemplated making a movie. Yes, of course, some of the guys on the course had talked about one day following through with what they learned.

It bugged me though, those words: *What's stopping you?* They rattled around and around in my head for ages and then one day, during meditation, I actually put it out there, why the hell not? Why couldn't I make a movie, what was stopping me?

I asked: "If the Universe believes that making a movie is the right thing for me to be doing then please place me in the right place at the right time for this to happen, if it is my Divine right."

Trust the Universe

Later that day, I had a call from Com O'Murchu, founder of Australian Film Base where we did the director training. Com wanted us to help him with running a weekend workshop.

Of course we said yes. This was a message from the Universe and I had heard it loud and clear.

We helped Com that weekend and connections were made, as you can imagine. Since then we have worked with some of these people in the making of many short films, a take on the *Survivor* TV reality show, and have collaborated to make a spiritual feature film.

Isn't it amazing how the Universe works? I firmly believe it lined up the course and the connections.

But in saying that, we would have needed to be open and ready for the learning or we would never have achieved all that we have. The Universe knew we were ready.

What was stopping me from making a movie? Myself, I stood in the way—my belief in myself. Belief in how far we had come with Rovick Productions. Fear-based limitations held me back.

The OMM Project was an amazing experience, but it wasn't giving me what I needed on a spiritual level.

If anything, it was confusing me even more, so I asked the Universe to provide me a teacher who could teach me more about spirituality in a way I could understand.

"In the end, we will conserve only what we love, we will love only what we understand, we will understand only what we are taught."

Baba Dioum

CHAPTER NINE
The Teacher

A few days later I was out networking and a wonderful woman came and sat beside me. Her name was Elizabeth Conway, and we got talking, as you do. When I asked her what she did, she said she was a Reiki master, tarot reader, clairvoyant and just to top it all off, she ran spiritual workshops. I just stood there, gobsmacked, embraced her in the most cherished hug and said: "Thank you, thank you, thank you, the teacher has arrived."

Before I left that event I had made an appointment to meet with Elizabeth. I had an overwhelming urge to have a reading and see where this could lead me.

There was no denying I had a choice to make. I could stay where I was, confused and full of doubt, or open the door and embrace this new phase of my life.

When I arrived home I was on such a high. I was talking fifty to the dozen about Elizabeth and what she did, and more than once I referred back to the other night when I asked the Universe to provide me a teacher.

"About time," he responded.

You've got to love Rodney and his nonchalant way. Rodney married into spirituality.

I told him when we met in 1985 that I was spiritually in tune, that I sensed things. Most of my choices were made on gut feelings and I knew that spirituality was going to be a big part of my life. He didn't say much back then, but he wasn't scared off by my talk of spirits, guides and angels. If I had known back then what I know now, I would never have believed it, not in a million years, but I digress.

Elizabeth welcomed me as a long lost friend. I felt as if I'd known her forever; there was a *knowing connection*. You know the feeling—it's like déjà vu, but with a deeper sense of connection. I sat at the table, the Tarot cards ready. Elizabeth expertly read my past; and identified with great certainty where I was right at that moment, with spot on, 110% accuracy. It was at that point that something unusual happened. She got a message from *her people* that was specifically for her. She thanked me profusely, apologizing at the same time, said that she would share her personal message after the reading, and continued to read my future.

Until now, her reading had been spot on, but all of a sudden the things she was saying were so farfetched that I believed the personal message she had received had thrown her and she was now way off track.

Trust the Universe

Her reading had uncovered some health issues and she offered to do some Reiki on me. I had never experienced Reiki, I was more than happy to give it a go. What I felt as she placed her hands over my body was an overwhelming sense of peace and relaxation. I wasn't sure if that sensation was from the Reiki or not, because I felt a sense of peace after the reading, but I didn't care—it felt great and that's all that mattered. I said my goodbyes and headed home.

I had completely forgotten to ask about her personal message, and thought she must have forgotten as well.

A few days later, Elizabeth called to thank me again for providing her with what she called the missing link. She proceeded to tell me that, after my reading, she put together the entire course notes that she needed to run a course, in fact she revealed that spirit had helped her write the notes. She proceeded to open The ISIS Vision Institute, and wanted to run a pilot program. She asked if I would like to be one of those first students. Wow, what an honor!

I became one of the first students at The ISIS Vision Institute and the course was called The Universal Laws and Principles for Business Success.

I was back on my spiritual journey, and this time the teacher arrived in their Divine time, not mine.

This gave me the confidence that this was the right path, at the right time, with the right teacher.

It wasn't long before business was back in flow.

Clients were calling, we were busy filming some really interesting events and I rejoiced in that calm chaos that made my days refreshingly interesting. I was feeling pretty damn pleased with myself. The ripple effect was in full swing.

The ISIS program exceeded my expectations. Not only did Elizabeth answer my questions on the spiritual realm and how spirituality can enhance our business, she also focused on the start-up issues that most businesses face, such as creating a business plan, understanding your finances and getting them under control.

In writing this book I asked Elizabeth if she could clarify her account of our very first meeting. This was her response:

"My memory of our first meeting was you being introduced as someone who had a spiritual TV channel.

"I know I didn't reveal that to you at the time, but much later. That is why I didn't tell you initially what I did, as I thought you were already *connected*.

"I was more than happy that you wanted a reading, little knowing that it would change my world.

"The Universe doesn't reveal all, as it does like to surprise us."

Even when Elizabeth told me some time later that she heard that I had a spiritual TV channel I didn't listen because it was so far left field that I almost choked laughing.

I was to learn that the Universe will drip-feed you what you need, but only at a time that you are ready to receive it. From my experience *they* talk

Trust the Universe

in riddles and very cryptically which is extremely frustrating at times.

"The secret of success in life is for a man to be ready for his opportunity when it comes."

Benjamin Disraeli

CHAPTER TEN

Doors Continue to Open

I was back on my spiritual path. I had been receiving messages from my spiritual advisers and I was now listening more closely. I was trusting that the Universe was taking me down the path that was divinely mine. I was constantly being told I was surrounded by love and protection, that *my people* were with me every step of the way. All I had to do was believe. Believe in myself and believe the Universe was looking after me.

Because of some charity filming work we did for a Rotary club, we were noticed by our local council, which in turn has bought in a lot of filming work.

On one particular day we received a phone call asking if we did live streaming. They had an event coming up for Literacy Week, where they would have about five people reading stories to two hundred school children live at a local library. They wanted the event streamed to twenty-six local schools so that the children in the classroom could watch it on their smart boards.

Interestingly enough, we had been asked to live stream an event some time earlier, but they hadn't given us enough time to get organized.

So, when this call came, we were already pretty savvy with the research and knew what equipment we had to get. Hence the answer to her question was a resounding yes. Luckily, we had a few months to get all the right equipment and test it before the big day.

The event went ahead without any problems and the feedback we received from council, the library, and the teachers was wonderful, but the feedback from the kids was the most enlightening. We heard that they were enjoying watching what was happening on the screen. When they saw their friends and schoolmates on the smart board, the experience became real and changed the dynamics and atmosphere in the classroom.

That was when we realized the power of the live streaming tool that we had successfully utilized.

A door had been opened and we began another journey, only this time it was a very powerful force toward our future and the future of Rovick Productions.

I felt a shift within: I was beginning to see possibilities. Rodney had already figured out some opportunities we could utilize immediately for our clients.

It was plainly obvious there was no stopping us now—we were on our way to bigger and better things.

We started live editing the events we were filming, which opened the eyes of our clients to

Trust the Universe

the technology we could provide. For me personally, it meant that I edited the event right there at the time of the event, so I just had to tidy it all up when I got back into the office, meaning turn-around time was so much quicker.

To be able to offer our clients the option of live streaming their event worldwide could potentially multiply their audience ten-fold. I'm sure you can relate to people who would love to attend an event, but can't make it due to circumstances either in or beyond their control. But, if they had the option to watch it either live from another location, or at a later date at their convenience, that could essentially triple potential sales.

This is the magic we hold in our hands right now. Last year, when the realization hit, we didn't know what to do with it. Sure, we had the technology, but how could we use it? We believed we had everything we needed to operate our own online TV station, but did we? Could we? How would we do it?

We were quick to tell people about filming their events via live stream, but the concept was relatively new and we struggled to get people as excited as we were.

I mentioned it a few times during meditation. I said: "I thank you for this amazing technology you have provided us. I am sure you have a plan for what you want us to do with it, but I am confused so please show me or tell me in a way that I can understand what you want me to do next."

Barbara Hayward, whom I had met a year earlier, had turned out to be the spiritual advisor for The OMM Project, but by the time she joined the project, I had left, so I didn't really get to work with her at that time.

But a funny thing did happen when Barbara provided a reading for me. Do you remember when Elizabeth Conway did my reading she was given a personal message from *her people* giving her the missing link. Well, the same thing happened with Barbara.

Barbara had been writing a book about her spiritual journey and, during my reading, she was told that we were the film crew that would make a feature film of her book. This revelation took her by surprise and left us totally gob-smacked.

Hells bells, a feature film, what next? OK, so we'd been the production house for three short films and crewed many more, but to make a feature film! This was serious stuff. We spent quite a few months discussing the different scenes, the plot, characters, location etc.

To date, this feature film is still in pre-production and is an excellent example of Divine timing.

What did occur, as a result of the connection that has formed with Barbara, was she asked us to film some interviews for her. She asked seven women who use spirituality in business to talk about their experiences. I was fortunate to be one of those women.

We filmed this over two days and had it set up so that I did the live editing. We used three cameras and made a point of making the clients feel totally comfortable and at ease before going on camera. Luckily, I knew most of the women,

Trust the Universe

but I met for the first time two highly spiritual women, Rosie Condo and Geraldine Teggelove.

When Geraldine entered the room, Barbara could tell immediately that Geraldine was given a message from *her people*. She wouldn't share what she was told at that moment, but did reveal later that we were on a winner with the TV station and she would be involved in some way, but *her people* wouldn't tell her how or when.

The next day Rosie was heard to say in relation to her interview with Barbara: "Yesterday I felt like I was on the Oprah Winfrey Show."

That's a pretty big shoe to fit, but if that is the intention the Universe has for us, then bring it on, I'm ready for the challenge.

This gave me the confidence that we were definitely on the right track, especially with references like that. You'd be bonkers if you couldn't see the Universe playing a major part in opening doors and connecting us to some key players.

"Happiness cannot be travelled to, owned, earned, or worn.

It is the spiritual experience of living every minute with love, grace & gratitude."

Denis Waitley

CHAPTER ELEVEN
Enlightenment

I knew my internal guidance system was working because I was in flow. Work was a breeze, doors were being opened and I was ready to walk through them, opportunities were arising from everywhere, and I knew I was being guided by Divine wisdom.

Even though I was in flow, I felt like I needed more spiritual guidance.

I wasn't sure what that should be, until I was out networking and came home with a business card for a local clairvoyant. I hadn't actually met Carmel Vassallo that night whilst networking, I had simply gone to get a drink and when I returned her business card was sitting on the table in front of me.

Rodney was going through a few problems at work and asked me if I could recommend a good clairvoyant. I gave him Carmel's business card and he went along for a reading.

Her reading was amazing and most of it

resonated with him. In all honesty, there were a few things that Carmel mentioned that he thought were pretty left field.

As I write this book, I just listened to his reading again, although it is now six months old.

The project he was about to do when he saw her that day, the one that was causing him so much grief, and the one he related to in her message about what he was going to do in the future, didn't actually happen in the way he had initially interpreted it.

But now, six months later, and listening to the recording again, I can see the chain of events he had to go through to bring him to where he is today, and that the message in the reading relates to the project he is working on at the moment, not the previous one.

Isn't it funny how the Universe works? You think one thing and firmly believe that's what's going to happen, but the Universe may indeed have another plan.

Sometimes it doesn't matter what you do or don't do, the Universe will deliver it to you when you are ready for it. This is yet another example of Divine timing.

I had a reading with Carmel about a month after Rodney. This was the first time I had met her. She didn't know me from a bar of soap.

There was no way she could connect me with Rodney or remember what she said to him the day he had his reading.

My reading was almost a duplicate to his; the only real difference was reference to my spiritual growth and what I should be focusing on.

Trust the Universe

The holidays were to the same places at around the same time. The health and family messages were the same. Work was much the same, but slightly different, because a lot happened in that month between readings, and Rodney and I focus on the business from different angles. She did tell me something that made me gasp for breath—I heard her, but didn't comprehend the exact interpretation of the message.

She said we would create a TV station, something online, something different, something that wasn't mainstream. She said our only competition would be Channel 7, which is one of the big players of mainstream TV here in Australia. When she said that, I sort of switched off—to interpret the possibility of that was beyond my comprehension.

Why would the Universe set me up to fail? I wondered.

I looked dumbfounded and asked her what I was supposed to do? She said, "They are telling me to tell you that if Oprah can do it, then so can you."

That set a fire in my belly that just wouldn't go out. What could I do that could possibly compare to Oprah and Channel 7? I had no idea.

That message is what I term as the slap-in-the-face the Universe gives you when they really want you to take notice. From past experience, they usually tell you something three times, and if you don't take notice, they take it that you aren't interested, you don't want it, or you aren't ready for it.

Can I say this is the fifth time over six months

that spiritual advisors had given me a similar message, and, as I said to Rodney when I got home, "Maybe we need to seriously start listening to what the Universe has in store for us, as scary as that may be."

I ramped up my spiritual training to include group meditation classes, which appeared at exactly the right time. Carmel mentioned at my reading that she ran a weekly meditation class that I could certainly benefit from, so I went along and soon became one of the regulars.

This was most definitely a case of when the student is ready, the teacher will appear.

A couple of days after I started the meditation class I was getting something out of the freezer when out of the blue came a message saying: "You will be compared to Oprah because you will give back to your guests and live audience like she does." That was all I heard, but it was also the third reference to Oprah in just a few short weeks, so maybe, just maybe, there was something to it all.

I picked up the phone and called Carmel to tell her what I heard.

She reassured me that we were definitely on the right track, our online TV station will be different to mainstream TV and it will be slow to start, but then it will take off and be seen globally and be compared to Oprah, because, like hers, our TV station will have a spiritual foundation.

Carmel also reassured me that the Universe was certainly backing us and we were protected. There was no need to worry; all I had to do was trust the Universe and trust in myself to deliver the end product.

No pressure!!!

We set about brain storming ideas for different shows. What would an audience watch and how could we fund it? What would our model look like? Where would we film it and whom did we know that we could do joint ventures or strategic alliances with?

The meditation classes were the perfect place for Rodney and me to attend.

This environment was where I could connect with *my people* and get a clear understanding of what was unfolding around me. The love and support of the class made the experience so much more rewarding.

"The spiritual path - is simply the journey of living our lives.

Everyone is on a spiritual path; most people just don't know it."

Marianne Williamson

CHAPTER TWELVE
Where the Magic Happens

Over the months that followed, we tweaked our model to fit the challenging issues we were facing and in the end decided that we just needed to get filming. We were stuck in a catch-22—we had a concept, but were having trouble getting possible investors or sponsors on-board, mainly because we didn't have anything to show them. To get an audience and grow a community we needed a couple of shows to prove we could do it.

It is just a matter of looking at each show individually and breaking it down into a format that could be replicated. Find a crew, a host, a venue to film and a budget or means of paying everyone.

We had learned a long time ago the value of one's time, and we wanted this TV station to be built on a foundation with values of respect, integrity, team work, ingenuity and creativity.

We knew we wanted to provide a platform for people who had a great idea for a show or had a unique story to tell that would never normally be given an opportunity to do so mainstream.

We want this TV station to be seen globally and on all devices, allowing everyone the opportunity to watch it. We want this TV station to be free, and it may still be, but until such time as funding comes from somewhere to pay the crew, the filming location, the social media, website and platform delivery then, unfortunately, this model will require that the audience pay to watch. In saying that, it will still be very, very, very affordable.

The first show is an interview-based show. Originally, we wanted both the guest and the host to be spiritual, but realized we were niching down too tightly and so now our criterion for this show is to interview open-hearted people doing extraordinary things.

We have already filmed a few different shows; we would like to trial some variety before we go live to a global audience starting early 2014.

We are in pre-production for three other shows and I know that once we go live we will be inundated with show ideas and that will be a wonderful problem to have.

We are in an amazing place right now, and I know I would never have arrived here had I not trusted the Universe, myself, my spiritual advisors and of course my wonderful crew.

I would not be here, living this amazing life, if my spiritual advisors had not constantly reminded me of my future, even when the messages were so outrageous that I couldn't comprehend them and didn't want to listen.

Trust the Universe

You never know, one day we may just give Channel 7 a run for their money, as was indicated by the Universe. Who knows? What I do know is anything is possible, and you should never underestimate what the Universe has in store for you.

Of course, I have not revealed all that the Universe has shared with me about my future.

That is purely because, like me, you would think it totally unbelievable. I certainly thought so when I heard most of the things I have been told over the last fifteen years.

Remember, way back in New Zealand in 2001 when Dorothy said we would move back to where we came from (Melbourne) and that Rodney and I would work together, that Rodney would invent something that would change our lives considerably? He may not have invented the platform that we are using to deliver the TV station, but he has put it all together as no one else would have.

Maybe, just maybe, what he is going to invent hasn't happened just yet.

At least, I'm open enough to know it's a possibility.

My future is a work in progress and I know that there is an easy and a hard way of doing business. I will always choose the easy way, and to do that I have to be in flow. To have it turn out the way I want, I know I have to be at one with the Universe and myself.

It's easy to identify when I am out of balance, because that's when life gets hard.

After reading this book, I wonder if you will be

more likely to listen to your intuition, gut feelings or take notice of the messages around you.

I am living proof that, when you trust the Universe, magic really does happen. The longer I stay connected to a heart-space full of self-belief, the Universe continues to deliver magical opportunities each and every day and for that I am extremely grateful.

"I like to believe that you don't need to reach a certain goal to be happy.

I prefer to think that happiness is always there, and that when things don't go the way we might like them to, it's a sign from above that something even better is right around the corner."

David Archuleta

CHAPTER THIRTEEN
Finally

This book told the journey of my life from July 2001 to September 2013. Since publishing this book, I have been constantly asked, 'What happened next?' and until now—November 2018—I wasn't sure how to capture all that has happened to me since and, to be honest, I would probably have to write that as another book entirely.

Would it surprise you if I was to say that after publishing this book, *my people* took me to places and provided opportunities I'd never thought possible and they continue to surprise and even shock me with what they deem as my future.

The answer to *What happened next?* is, in a nutshell, me. Who I grew into as a person. The words of Teilhard de Chardin describe me perfectly:

"We are not a human being, having a spiritual experience. We are a spiritual being, having a human experience."

contributors

I personally thank everyone listed below for their direct or indirect inspiration and guidance. Thank you, thank you, thank you.

Barbara Hayward, Clairvoyant and Spiritual Advisor

http://barbaradhayward.com

Helena Steel, author of After Ansett

www.afteransett.com

Derek Barker, author of A Gift of Gratitude journal

www.derekbarker.com

Tom T Moore, author of The Gentle Way

www.thegentlewaybook.com

Carmel Vassallo, clairvoyant/spiritual advisor

Sharon Pearson, founder and director of The Coaching Institute

http://www.thecoachinginstitute.com.au

Elizabeth Conway, founder and director of ISIS Vision Institute

www.isisedu.org

Louise Hay, author and founder of Hay House Publications

www.louisehay.com

Doreen Virtue, author and self-proclaimed Spiritual Doctor of Psychology

www.angeltherapy.com

Diana Cooper, author and founder of Diana Cooper School of Angels and Ascension

www.dianacooper.com

Gary Schuller, founder and director of Breyk Throo Events

www.breakthroughevents.com.au

Jacqueline Bignell, founder and director of The Difference

www.thedifference.tv

Debra Wylde, founder and director of The OMM Project

www.ommproject.com

Heather Yelland, founder and director of Well Within Me

www.wellwithinme.com

Colm O'Murchu, founder and director of Australian Film Base

www.australianfilmbase.com

Memory of Your Life

Memory of Your Life is a step-by-step workbook designed to help you share your life stories with loved ones.

This simple, easy-to-use workbook gently guides you through life's most important memories and helps you record and share them in fine detail with poise, passion and purpose. It gives you opportunity to write anything left unsaid and to give insights into the real you.

When Vicki began showing people this step-by-step workbook concept it became evident that many people resonated with it. They felt the same way, recognising the need for a platform, like this workbook, to encourage people to record their stories and share them with family and friends.

Deadly Deception

Deadly Deception came about quite by chance. An avid fan of crime stories herself, Vicki embarked on a journey of mystery, revealing even she didn't know who did it until she wrote the words. She describes the writing process by saying that once she 'got out of the way' the characters took over and revealed their individual involvement in the crime.

The story is set on Clairemont Island, a secluded island in the South Pacific. Breathtakingly beautiful, this island has many a story to tell. The lies, deceit and secrets of the residents and holidaymakers will make your hair curl.

When a crime is committed, it's up to the residents to race against time to uncover the murderer before a cyclone hits the island and potentially destroys all evidence.

Nobody is beyond suspicion.

A Deathly Shade of Passion

A Deathly Shade of Passion is the second in the Clairemont Island Mystery series.

Tension builds when a magazine crew arrives from LA for a photo shoot. Having to source local talent seems easy at first. One person's life depends on their secret being kept under wraps; however, a chance encounter brings past crimes into the spotlight.

The heady mix of L.A personalities and locals ignites a whole storm of passion and intrigue. Around them, all hell breaks loose when pride and ego erupt, causing a catastrophic outcome.

Some of the fascinating, scheming and wild characters from *Deadly Deception* appear here in a menacing romp through an increasingly sinister paradise.

About the Author

Vicki Williams

Author of Trust the Universe

Author of Memory of Your Life

Author of Deadly Deception

Author of A Deathly Shade of Passion

New Zealand born Vicki Williams lives in Australia. Vicki has always had a passion to write, but lacked the confidence to do anything more with her stories. That was until she entered a challenge to write a book in forty hours and shocked herself by producing her first book '**Trust the Universe**'.

Vicki has successfully taken other authors from story conception to publication as she mentors and teaches 'How to Write' workshops in person and online.

Vicki continues writing the Clairemont Island mystery series, as well as a young adult series written under the pen name of Jade Green. With a drawer full of possible storylines, it will be interesting to see where she leads us in the future.

"We are shaped by our thoughts; we become what we think.

When the mind is pure, joy follows like a shadow that never leaves."

Buddha

"Always say 'yes' to the present moment...
Surrender to what is.

Say 'yes' to life and see how life starts suddenly working for you rather than against you."

Eckhart Tolle

www.ingramcontent.com/pod-product-compliance
Lightning Source LLC
Chambersburg PA
CBHW020659300426
44112CB00007B/454